BEAUTIFUL THOUGHTS

Everyday Reflections on a Good Life

Written by Miriam Hathaway
Designed by Emily Carlson

With the
new day comes
new strength and
new thoughts.

Eleanor Roosevelt

WHAT DOES IT MEAN TO HAVE BEAUTIFUL THOUGHTS?

It's when you consciously add goodness to your day, whether it's a pause to reflect, a chance for inspiration, or a shift in perspective. Beautiful thoughts change your mindset, which can change how you act, which can change your life.

This book is here for you to take a moment and discover new ways to create your own beautiful thoughts. It's a place to anchor your intention to nurture a heart-led life. It takes practice, but it's somewhere you can return to again and again.

To start, take a long, deep breath, quiet your mind, and choose any page you like...

Life is a beautiful, magnificent thing…

Charlie Chaplin

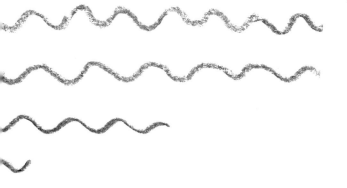

That first sip of coffee or tea in the morning.
Slipping into a warm bath. Stepping barefoot
into a mountain stream on a hot day. Such
moments of pure bliss happen all the time,
every day of our lives—moments that wake up
the deepest parts of ourselves, connecting us
to the privilege of just being here right now.
These thresholds of newness are constantly
here to remind us, but sometimes we forget
to notice. Pausing to savor them lets us fully
experience the gifts of today.

Find wonder
in all things,
even the most
commonplace.

Carl Linnaeus

When you look at something under a magnifying glass, you notice small details you wouldn't otherwise see. A sidewalk may seem ordinary, but looking closely you find pebbles as varied as precious gems. A polished, marbled green one. A speckled, robin's-egg blue. Maybe a heart-shaped one. Then a single black ant rushes by. A dandelion seed tumbles along a low wind. An extraordinary world within an ordinary landscape. Miraculous beauty is always around you, ready for you to look closely, ready to spark your curiosity and sense of awe.

What the
heart remembers
most are moments
shared.

Elizabeth Browne

You're making a dish to bring to a potluck. You know that if you were just feeding yourself, that big bowl of coleslaw would not make a very exciting meal all on its own. But when you arrive, there are colorful fruits, warm biscuits, chips and dip, fresh sliced veggies, and a cheesy casserole. Together you've made a feast. These are the moments when you feel the most connected with others, when you are providing fulfillment for each other and sharing in the beauty of the day. You're giving *and* receiving as one.

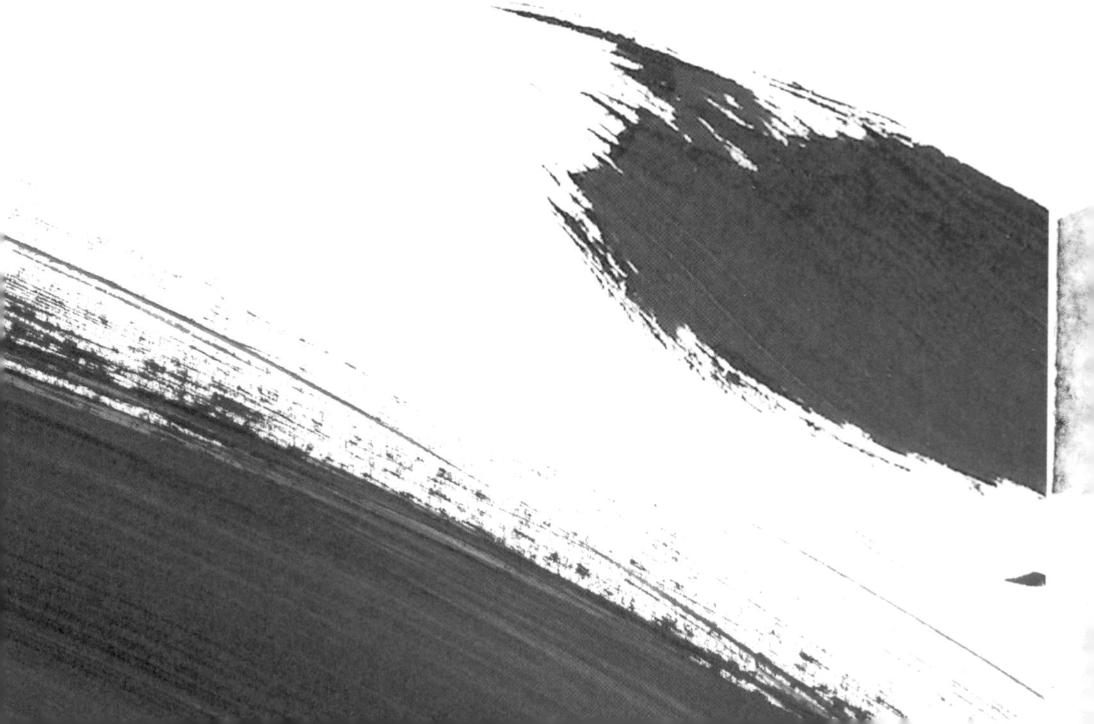

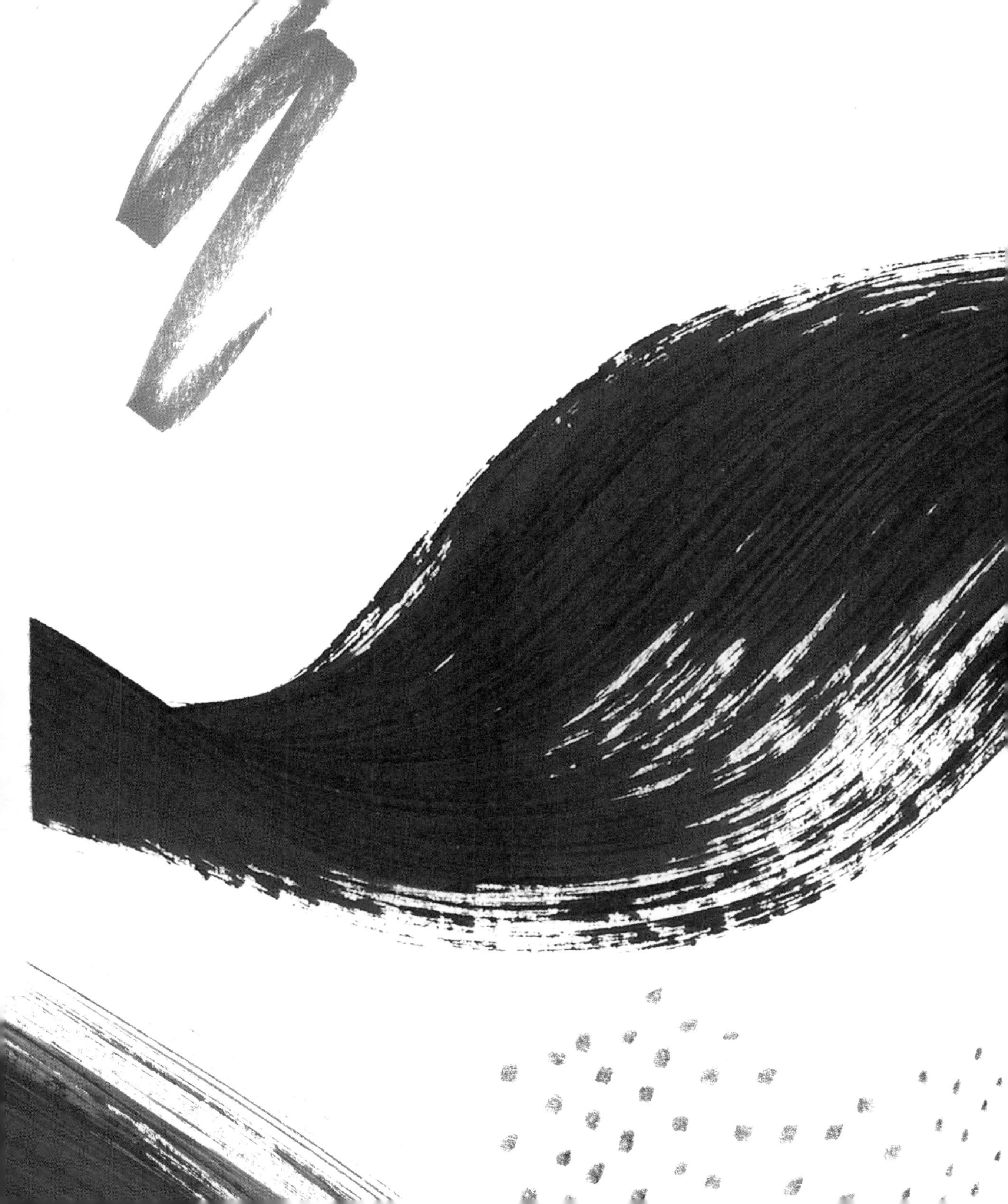

A possibility was born the day you were born and it will live as long as you live.

Marcus Solero

———————

Having a deeper belief in what's possible can radically change everything. Because it's true—you can do anything. But to visualize your full potential is only the beginning. The next thing is to create steps to get there. Then follow them. It's just like a dance. You'll make some mistakes along the way, but you keep learning the moves as you go. With enough rehearsal, you'll get the beat down.

> The happy heart gives away the best.

Dhyani Ywahoo

Offering more than what's expected extends your happiness out into the world around you. It ripples and multiplies when you give freely and abundantly to your loved ones, friends, neighbors, and strangers. Even if the only gift you have to offer is your full presence, your complete attention, you've contributed something invaluable. A generous heart gives with respect and humility. It gives from a place of pure goodness. And it's through this intention that we show our deepest gratitude.

Because of your smile, you make life more beautiful.

Thich Nhat Hanh

———————————

You pass by another person on the street. They're
walking fast, clearly in a hurry. Maybe they're on the
phone talking to someone else. You meet their gaze
and smile. Chances are they'll smile back, because
smiles are contagious. In that moment, you have
relieved a little stress for both of you, maybe even
lowered your blood pressure. You made a human
connection that wasn't there before. In that small,
yet significant moment, your smile added a touch
of radiance to the world.

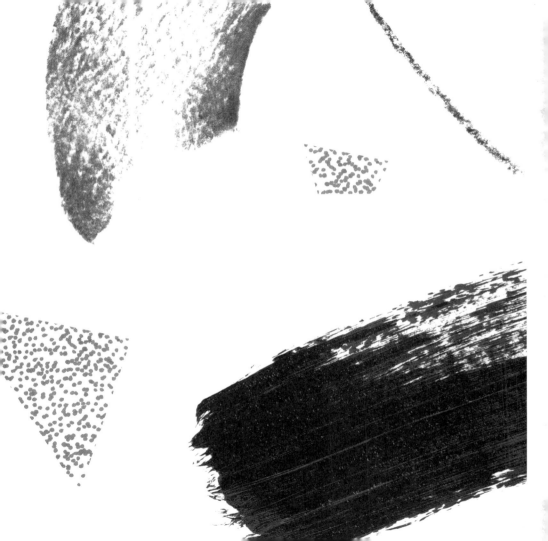

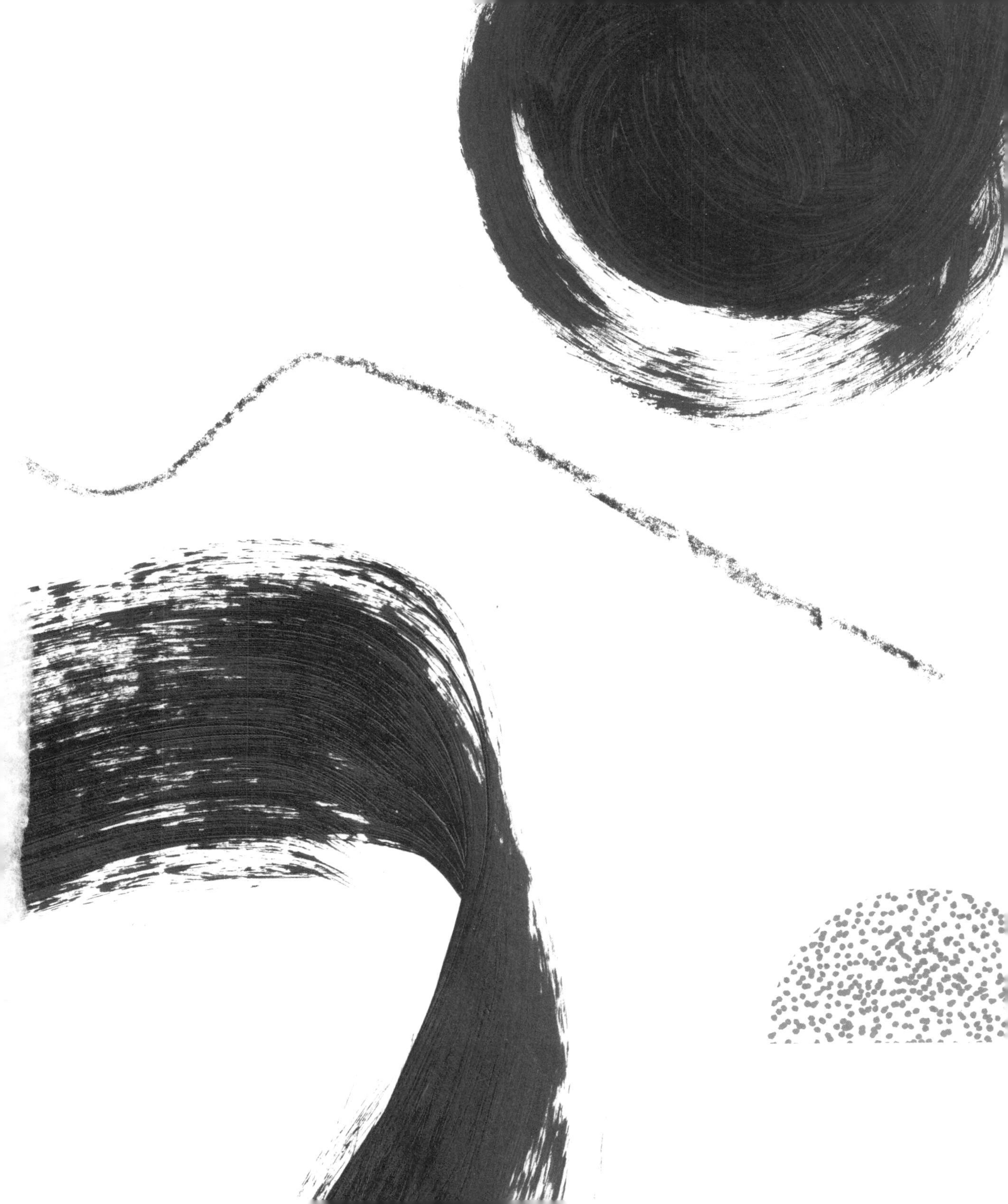

...WE HAVE WHAT WE SEEK. WE DON'T HAVE TO RUSH AFTER IT. IT IS THERE ALL THE TIME, AND IF WE GIVE IT TIME IT WILL MAKE ITSELF KNOWN TO US.

Thomas Merton

As children, we are constantly learning how to wait. Waiting in line with a parent at the grocery store, trying not to squirm too much. Waiting our turn on the swings at the park. Waiting for grandparents to finally arrive for a visit. Waiting is often hard and emotional, and can be full of frustration and anxiety. When we practice mindful patience, waiting calmly even in the face of adversity and mistakes, we are given the time to prepare for all the good that is coming. We learn how to wait throughout our lives, and with each opportunity rediscover that persistent patience reveals its own gifts to us.

Know that
there is
something
inside you
that is
greater than
any obstacle.

Christian D. Larson

Some things are clearly courageous. Firefighters rushing into a fire. Singing a solo in front of a large crowd. Skydiving for the first time. Yet there are a multitude of everyday, unpraised moments of courage. Going to the gym after a long absence. Starting a new job. Learning to drive as an adult. Doing something brave means something different to you than it does to anyone else. It's facing your own unique fears, practicing your ability to endure. You may be afraid, but the thing you dread is infinitely smaller than the will of your heart.

This is a
wonderful day.
I've never seen
this one before.

Maya Angelou

———————

Looking down a greeting card aisle, you can easily spot significant life milestones: birthdays, graduations, weddings. A new home, a new baby, a new job. We acknowledge the big things, which instills good memories for years to come. So why don't we celebrate every day with that same sense of wonder? Why not high-five your neighbor for the first tomato in their garden? Or sing a song when you find the perfect pair of jeans? Find something worth celebrating in everything.

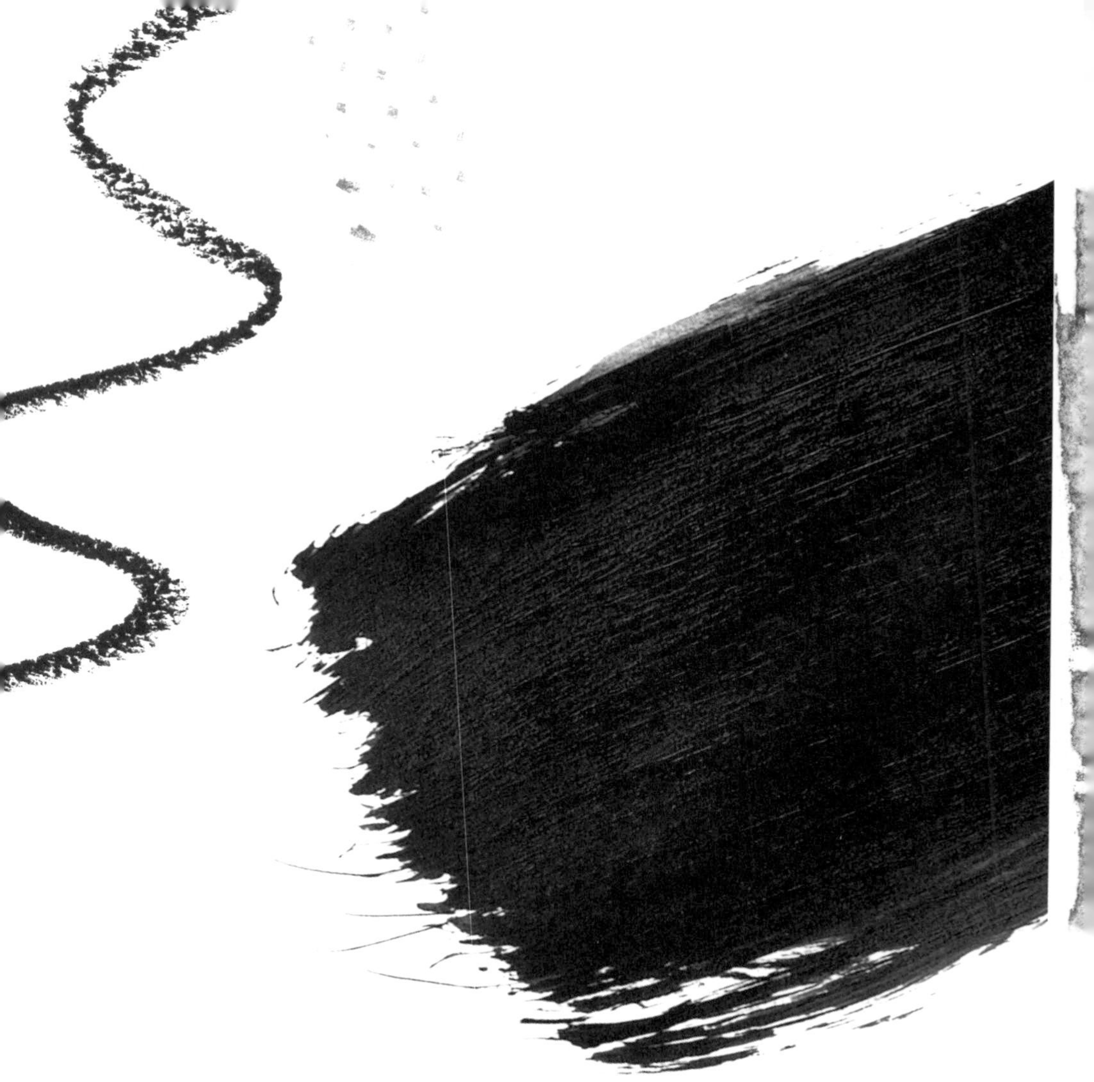

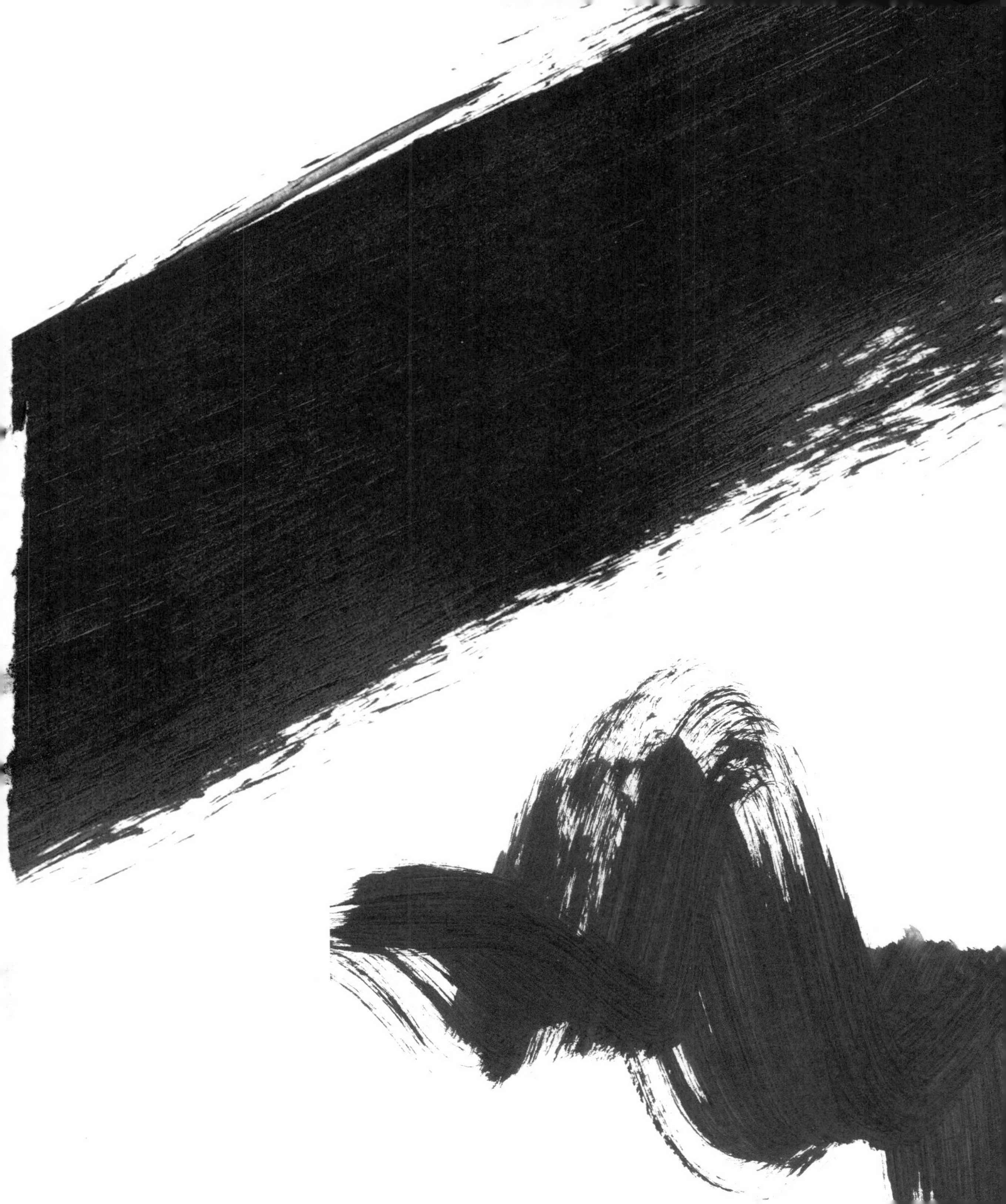

"

If you truly put your
heart into what you
believe in, even if it
makes you vulnerable,
amazing things can
and will happen.

Emma Watson

———————

It's often easier to melt into the crowd than show off the things that set us apart. But those are the very things that can be our strength. Being authentically you and showing your vulnerabilities isn't being weak, but being beautifully human. Let your soft spots show. Honor your unique dreams and experiences. Live by your strengths. We all have fears and flaws that fight to hold us back, but when you stand before them with courage, you'll shine brighter than you ever thought possible.

"

...thanks are the highest form of thought; and that gratitude is happiness doubled by wonder.

G. K. Chesterton

A grateful heart bonds us with others. When we give thanks, we recognize the gift we've received and the giver. We're grateful for the hand-knit hat and our friend who made it. We're grateful for the fresh apples at the farmers market and the farmer who grew them. You can even take it a step further. You're grateful for the sheep that gave the wool to spin the yarn. For the apple tree that bears the fruit. Giving thanks invites us to get curious about the world and to acknowledge all the many connections we have within it.

Let the rays
of your heart
shine on all
who pass by.

Terri Guillemets

One of our deepest human desires is to be seen and understood by others. It becomes especially poignant when we are in pain. When you witness someone in need, you have a chance to give one of your greatest gifts: compassion. That's why a simple recognition, such as a smile or a wave, connects you with others in a meaningful way. You're practicing your ability to understand someone else, to offer a healing gesture, and to share a moment of respect for each other.

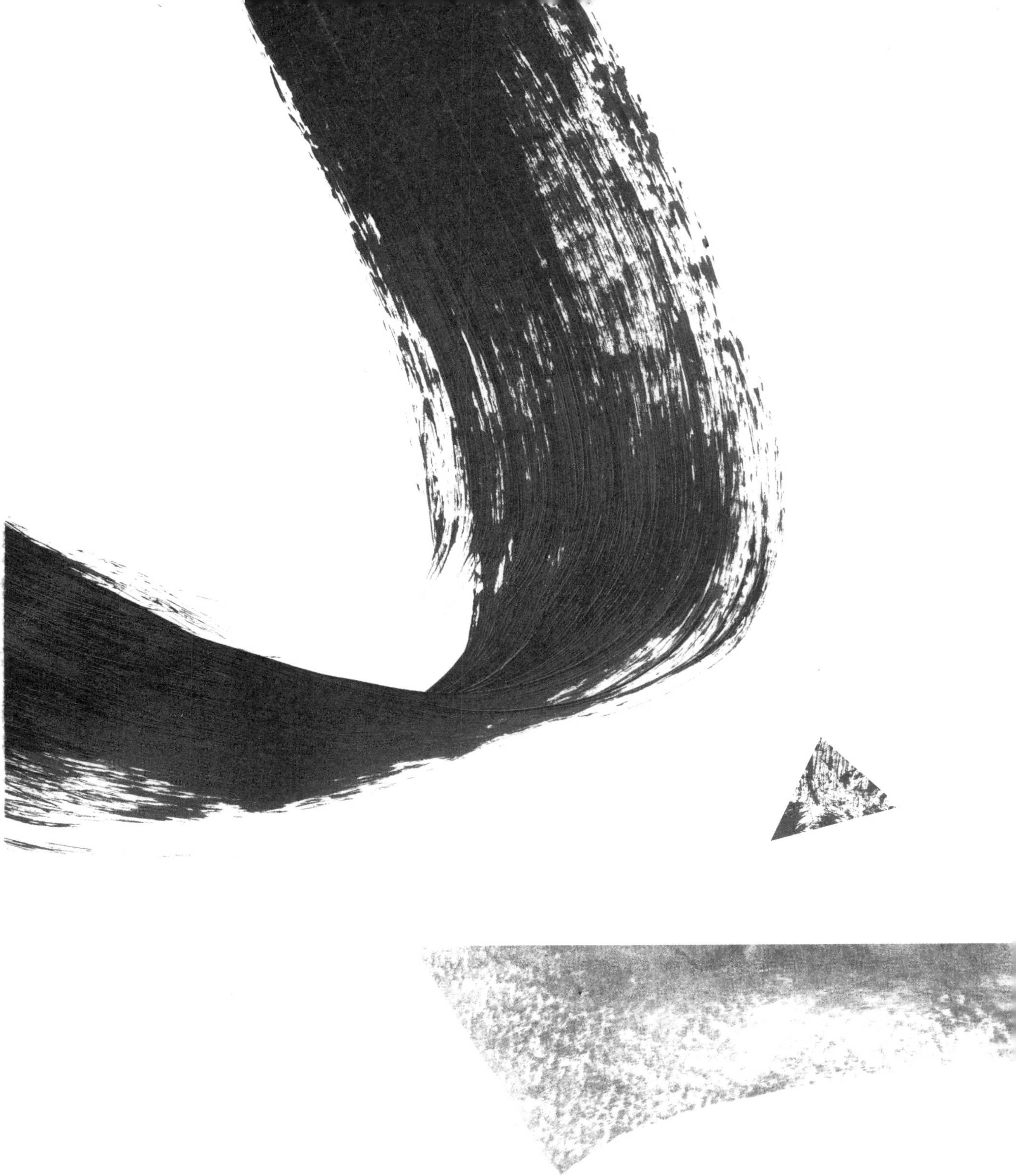

EVERY DAY OF
OUR LIVES WE ARE
ON THE VERGE OF
MAKING THOSE
SLIGHT CHANGES
THAT WOULD MAKE
ALL THE DIFFERENCE.

Mignon McLaughlin

Remember when you first learned how to ride a bike? It took practice. It took time. You had to learn to balance your body on the seat, pedal in a synchronized beat, steer the handlebars with your hands and arms. It took your whole body and mind working together to figure it out, but when you did, something clicked. You practiced resilience. Perseverance. Your success isn't driven by talent alone, but by your determination to keep trying, to keep showing up to learn, to self-correct, and to be ready for anything.

Sometimes the most important thing in a whole day is the rest we take between two deep breaths...

Etty Hillesum

There's something almost magical that happens when we rest. Our minds slow down. Our bodies renew. We simply feel better. Being mindful of relaxing, and all the good things it provides, deepens our overall experience. Just like how the muscles in your body grow stronger after a workout, you also gain greater strength when you take the time—if only for a bit—to slow down. Pausing, noticing the spaces in which to unwind, even if it's just for a moment, allows you to move throughout the day rooted in peace.

...prepare your mind to receive the best that life has to offer.

Ernest Holmes

Having a positive attitude is not the same as being naively upbeat. It's encouraging yourself and others around you, getting curious about the unknown, or telling someone they've done a great job. It's having fun even if you're losing. It's trying again and committing yourself over and over again. These are the building blocks to ensuring success. This is how you can anticipate, and witness, your dreams coming true.

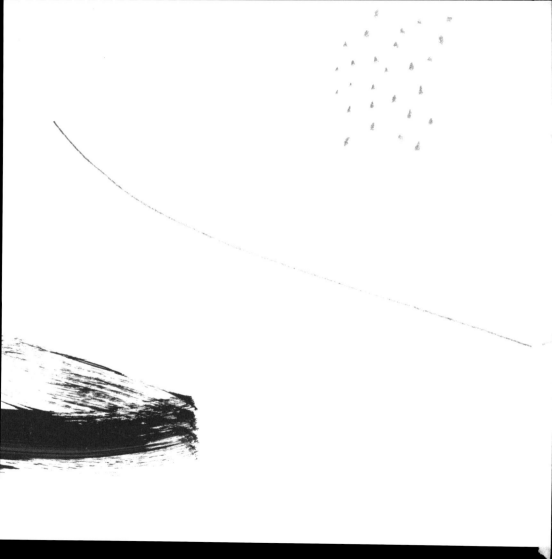

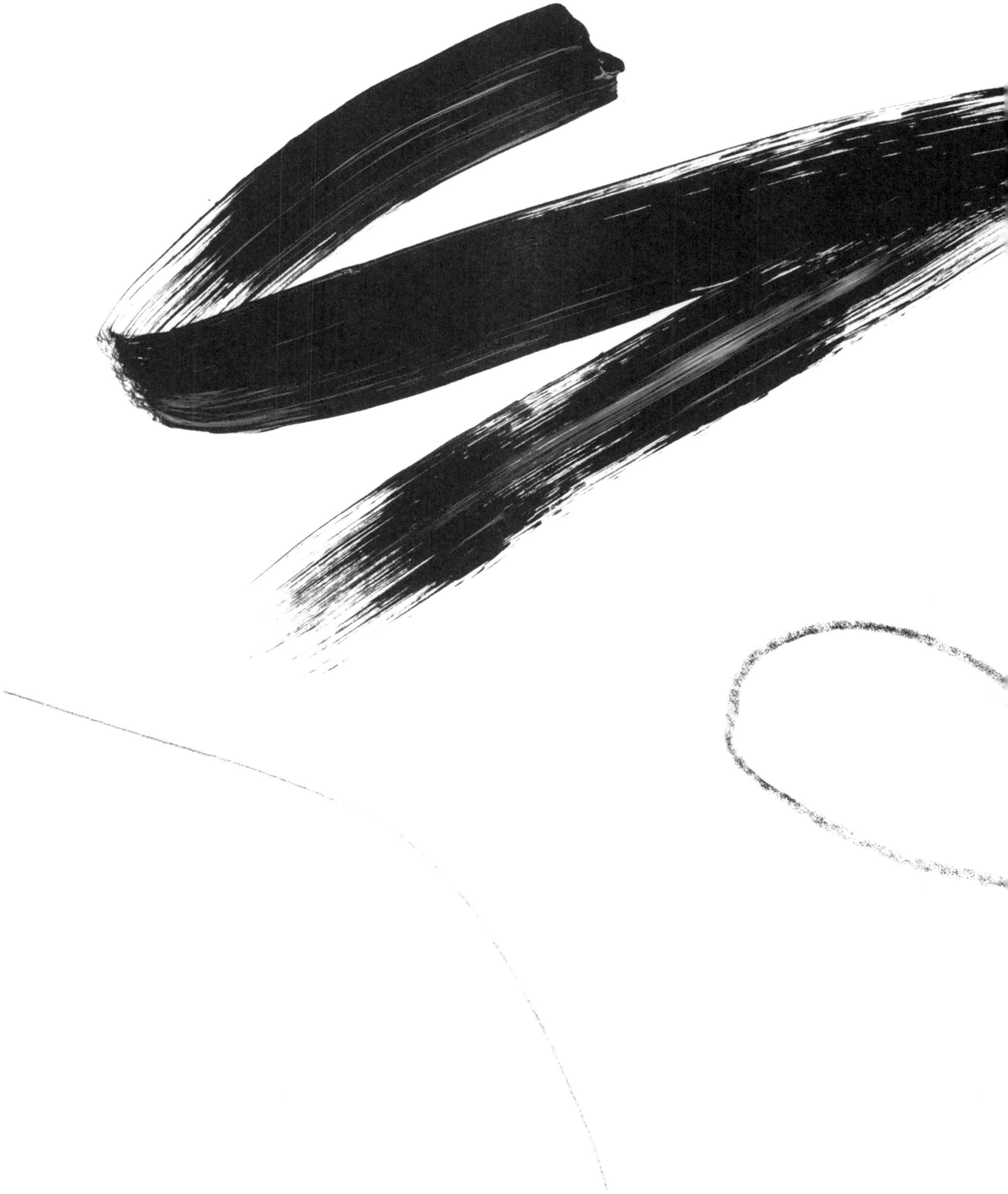

Surround yourself
with people who make
you hungry for life,
touch your heart, and
nourish your soul.

Unknown

———————

Friendships anchor us to a more mindful, connected life. We rebound quicker from life's setbacks through the support of friends—and we delight more fully in life's good times when they're shared. It's why we instinctively hold hands before we jump into a pool together. Why we cheer when a pal makes the winning shot. Why we hug when we see each other for the first time in a while. Friendships nurture us, help us grow, and enrich our lives, because we are better together than we are alone.

Let the winds of enthusiasm sweep through you. Live today with gusto.

Dale Carnegie

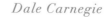

Having a zest for life doesn't come naturally to all of us. In fact, some of us seem hardwired to find the negative in any situation, criticizing and complaining our days away. Now think of the people in your life who you find most joyful. A friend who is always willing to try something new. A coworker who encourages everyone else. They can be irresistible to be around. Magnetic. This is enthusiasm at work. Find that passion for life in choosing happiness, accepting the risks, and doing it anyway. It's what moves you ahead.

Everything
you can imagine
is real.

Pablo Picasso

Your mind can come up with an image of a rainbow, just like that. You see the bright stripes of color: red, orange, yellow, green, blue, and purple arched across the sky like a dramatic brushstroke. It may not be in view right now, but you can see it just the same. Just like how you know that the Eiffel Tower exists, even if you haven't seen it for yourself. Believe in the good things your imagination has to tell you. Believe in the dreams that it makes. There is real power in possibility.

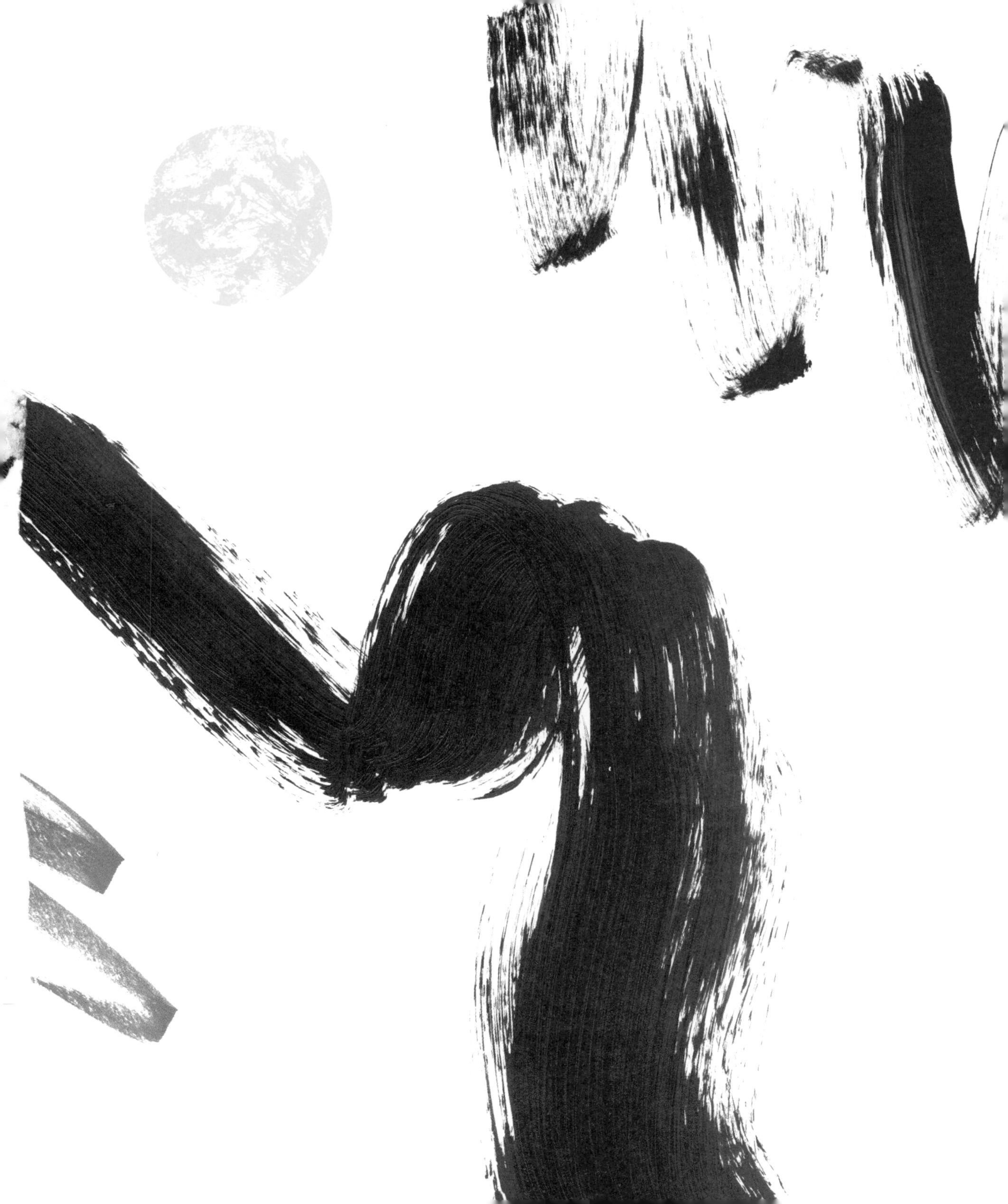

BE CONTENT WITH
WHAT YOU HAVE;
REJOICE IN THE
WAY THINGS ARE.
WHEN YOU REALIZE
THERE IS NOTHING
LACKING, THE
WHOLE WORLD
BELONGS TO YOU.

Lao-tzu

It's impossible to be happy all the time, but you can find contentment within each moment. Dissatisfaction comes from thinking we don't have something we think we need. Plus, we naturally place more value on the things we *don't* have and less on what we *do* have. So set yourself up for success and honor the best of you, as you already are, with what you already have, and lead with confidence.

> "

Kind thoughts, kind words, kind deeds, how brightly they always shine...

Mary Anderson

Happiness comes from loving and taking care of others, from discovering and sharing the warmth within. The good news is this: you always have people in your life who love and depend on you. Nurture them with care and affection, and they will return it to you. Then see beyond your own world and notice others in need. Open a door, carry a heavy load, say thank you, or share a homemade meal. We all want to be loved and nurtured, and your community depends on you just as you need them.

Keep some room
in your heart for
the unimaginable.

Mary Oliver

Not long ago, we all thought it was absurd to think we'd be walking around with phones in our pockets. Before that, we thought for sure that flying was just for the birds. It's true: by definition, impossible things can't happen. But things *thought to be* impossible can happen. Staying open to possibility, to a question, means keeping an eye on our most common assumptions. Thinking creatively, being creative, is not based on reality, but in imagining a brand-new reality for everyone to enjoy.

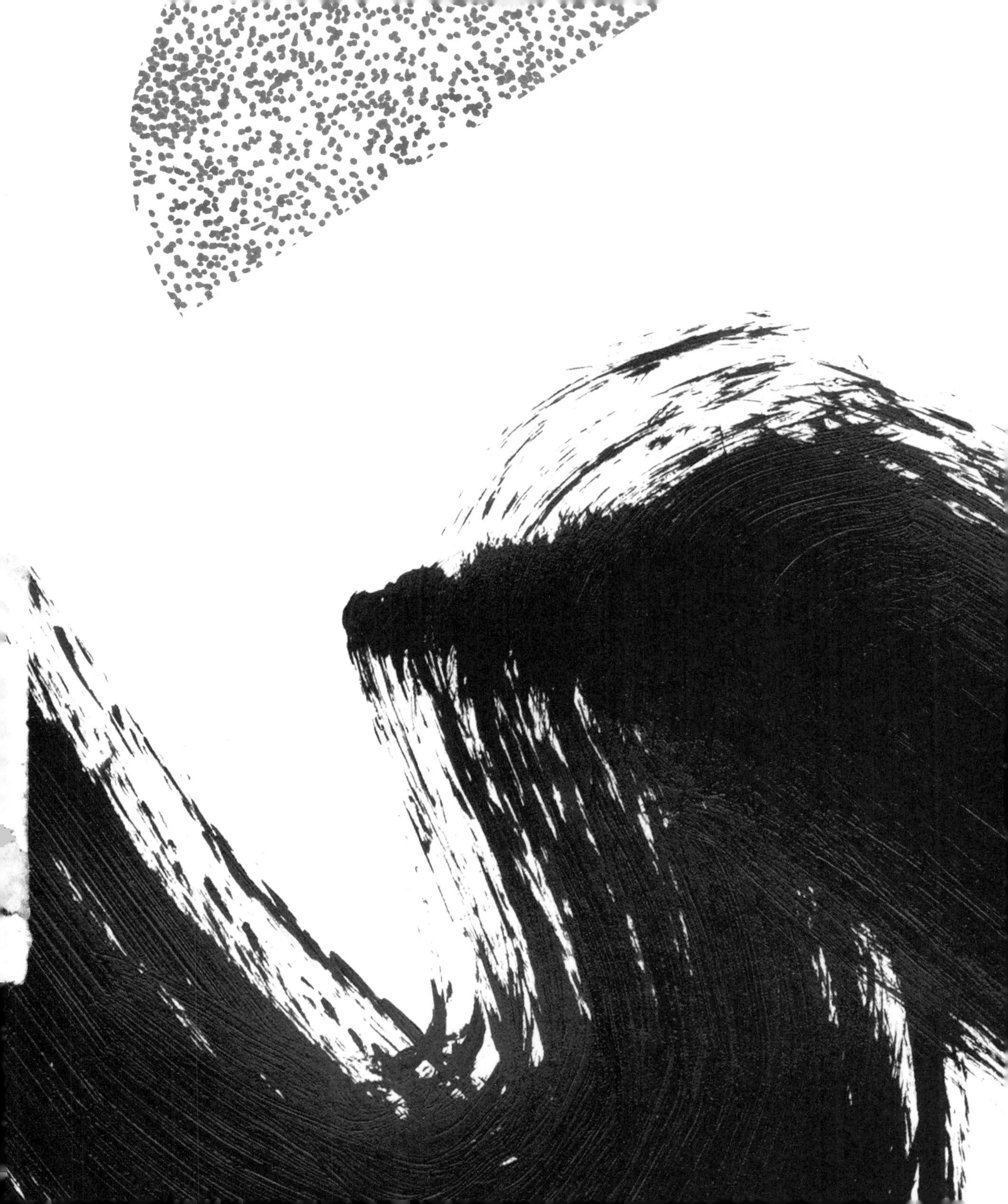

Look back in forgiveness, forward in hope, down in compassion, and up with gratitude.

Zig Ziglar

Throughout life's many experiences, we mess up and make mistakes. This often leads to sorrow, stress, or feeling lost. But you *can* learn from the past and, at the same time, take steps toward healing, growth, and happiness. Looking in every direction of your life, let go of grudges, let go of bitterness and resentment. Allow yourself to see the good, expect the good, and be the good. You'll create a compass for peace that leads you to deeper satisfaction and joy.

COMPENDIUM.
live inspired

Written by: Miriam Hathaway
Designed by: Emily Carlson
Edited by: Cindy Wetterlund

Library of Congress Control Number: 2019948206 | ISBN: 978-1-970147-03-2

2nd printing. Printed in China with soy inks on FSC -Mix certified paper.

*Create
meaningful
moments
with gifts
that inspire.*

CONNECT WITH US
live-inspired.com | sayhello@compendiuminc.com

   @compendiumliveinspired
#compendiumliveinspired